Ghostly
Encounters
South-West

Peter Underwood

Bossiney Books

*For my wife Joyce, with much love and
eternal gratitude for sharing with me
several ghostly encounters*

This reprint 2011

First published 1992. This abridged edition first published 2002 by
Bossiney Books Ltd, 33 Queens Drive, Ilkley, LS29 3QW
www.bossineybooks.com

ISBN 1-899383-49-2

Acknowledgements
The author gratefully acknowledges the help he has received in preparing
this volume and the permissions to quote from, among others, Donald
Armstrong, MBE, Gary Bissell, Mrs Marianne Burge, David Crawford, Lisa
Crawford, Miss C Curthoys, Miss Catherine Edwards, Lorraine Fisher,
Michael Goss, Mrs Patricia A Hall, Martin Kelsey, Win and Harry Kilbey,
Margery and Barry Knowles, Roger Little, Jamie Owen, Jon Pertwee,
Mrs C Piper, Chief Inspector J Sait, Alexandra Scull, George Smith,
ET Smith, Paul Soulsby, Miss NA Thorn; also the Exeter *Express and Echo*
and other local newspapers and periodicals.

Printed in Great Britain by R Booth Ltd, Penryn, Cornwall

To see a ghost…

If you crave a ghostly encounter you could not do better than visit the South-West of Britain: Cornwall, Devon and Somerset are a truly magical part of the country.

This selection of true ghost stories includes encounters with full seemingly-solid apparitions and with glimpses of shadowy forms; even with sounds of something unseen – just as mystifying and puzzling and frightening to the people present.

All represent ghostly encounters that defy explanation and remind us that occasionally, and perhaps especially in this mysterious, evocative and surprising area where the unexpected often happens, there are influences, forces and powers about which we know little and over which we have no control. If you happen to be in the right place at the right time you will experience something; you do not have to believe in such things, you do not have to be a certain type of person, you do not have to be of any particular age, sex, religion, race or belief – these happenings are reported by every kind and type of person from every part of the world – but especially from the Westcountry.

I quote, almost at random, from a letter sent to me by Mrs Patricia Hall of Bristol in August 1991: 'My husband and I, two years ago, together with my son and his wife, stayed with friends in Penzance. They had purchased a rambling house [but perhaps I should not describe or locate the house exactly]… My husband and I shared a twin-bedded room and in the middle of the night I awoke very suddenly, icy cold, with the distinct impression of someone sitting on the end of my bed. I felt a weight beside my feet and experienced a slight bouncing sensation, exactly as you would if someone had sat heavily down beside you. I became increasingly frightened and could feel the hairs stand up on the back of my neck but, regretfully, I did not have the courage to look…

'I managed to awaken my husband and together we looked and, needless to say, we saw nothing; and he laughed at my foolishness, but I had very little sleep for the rest of our stay.

'It was only recently that I told my son about it and instead of making fun of me he said that on the numerous occasions when he had stayed there while on business in Cornwall, he had experienced the identical thing; but he had never said anything to his hosts for fear of offending them...'

One day at the Savage Club in London I talked with Jon Pertwee, the actor and comedian, perhaps best known for his television role as Doctor Who, about a ghostly encounter which he shared with his brothers in Devon when they were young.

The Pertwees had a country house in Devon and while it was being extended the boys stayed at a little workman's cottage nearby – actually two cottages knocked into one with two downstairs sitting-rooms and two bedrooms. When their father went out in the evenings he used to say, 'You boys will be all right?' and they'd say, 'Yes, of course, we're fine.' Jon was sleeping in one bedroom with his stepbrother and there was a door through into the other bedroom where Michael, later to become a playwright and author, slept.

There was no television in those days and the cottage did not possess a radio, so after a few games of Mah Jong or draughts the boys usually turned in soon after nine o'clock. They were always relieved when their father came back to the house later to see that they were all right. He used to let himself in, come up the stairs and quietly open the door and then walk through into the next room to see that Michael was all right; then he'd go back downstairs and out of the back door. All the children liked to know that he checked on their well-being; it made them feel loved and wanted.

Then one evening when their father was going out to dinner with friends some miles away, the boys thoughtfully said to him,

'There's no need to come back to the house tonight, Dad, we'll be perfectly all right.' Their father looked at them rather strangely. 'What are you talking about?' he asked. 'Why should I come back?'

'Well, you usually do,' they said. And he replied, 'But I've never, ever come back here again after I've left you boys alone.' There was no explanation but equally there was no doubt that the three boys had heard someone – or some thing – clump up the stairs, pass through one room and go into the second; and then back down the stairs and out of the back door. All three boys simultaneously heard the sounds, quite clearly, and there was no doubt in their minds it was their father, but in fact on no occasion at those times had he been anywhere near the house.

Jon Pertwee added, sensibly, that there was no electricity in the wilds of Devon in those days and it was pitch dark, so none of the boys had actually seen anything odd when the 'presence' had visited them. But they were all satisfied that they must have had a ghostly encounter in Devon in the early 1930s, when the only artificial light was gaslight and oil lamps. Oddly enough, after their father told them he never returned at night to the cottage, they did not hear the ghostly footsteps again and soon afterwards they moved back to the house, with lasting memories of a ghostly visitation that had been accepted as normal.

The Westcountry means many things to many people. Just about everyone who visits these mystical and magical regions comes away with memories that last a lifetime – and not infrequently with a personal ghostly encounter that widens the horizons of experience and leaves a lasting, vivid and often moving and poignant memory in the reaches of the mind.

Peter Underwood
The Savage Club
1 Whitehall Place
London SWIA 2HD

The one-eyed miller – Boscastle, Cornwall

In 1991 my wife and I spent a week at Boscastle and while we were there we heard about a one-eyed man who was supposed to haunt the Old Mill next door to the Wellington Hotel where we were staying. We talked to the proprietors of the Old Mill, Margery and Barry Knowles (the building is now used as a craft centre), Win and Harry Kilbey, who used to run a café and disco there, and Roger Little, the local potter and a mine of information on Boscastle; we also talked to one or two other inhabitants who had knowledge of the ghost of the Old Mill.

Long referred to locally as 'that haunted place', the mill had once been worked by a one-eyed miller who died amid rumours of being a murderer and having hidden 'something' somewhere in the building.

Once, a girl occupying a flat in the old building awoke suddenly to find a dark figure bending over her, a man with one eye. When she screamed the figure vanished. Later she glimpsed the same figure in daylight when it disappeared into a solid wall in the basement of the building, where the old mill workings were once housed.

Win and Harry Kilbey, retired psychiatric nurses, both experienced odd happenings during their sojourn at the Old Mill. There was the night Harry heard footsteps and the sound of falling sand in the roof area; no reason was ever discovered for these and other strange sounds. One visitor said he had heard 'someone walking about all night...'

Win, very busy one mid-day during the August rush in the café, went down to the basement, needing something from the deep-freeze stored there and she found, for a split second, that the whole basement area had returned to what it had been years previously – a working mill! As she opened the door to the basement there was the mill working as it had done in the lively days of the one-eyed miller; the next moment everything had returned to normal and Win began to think she must have imagined it – but she knew she hadn't and she told us she can still remember seeing all the old machinery working away.

From time to time the lights in the Old Mill would go on by themselves. Several times the police were called, but there was no sign of an entry and nothing had been taken or disturbed. The lights in the dark, empty and locked building, however, had been switched on by 'something' – the one-eyed miller perhaps?

Once Harry Kilbey spent some time fixing cotton across the stairs and doorways and taping light switches, but it made no difference; a few hours later he was called out again and the police accompanied him as he unlocked and opened the doors of the Old Mill and there were the lights all blazing away and otherwise everything as he had left it, including the cotton and tapes still intact.

Doors, one in particular, would open and close without human contact and once Win saw a figure appear through the wall in the basement. She told me she couldn't really describe it, it all happened so quickly but it could have been a man in a smock, like a miller... The self-opening door was 'fixed' several times and by different people but it made no difference. Although there was no wind and the door had been re-hung and the latch checked and re-checked, no sooner did one walk away than the door would slowly open or, when left open for a moment, it would softly and quietly close. Someone or something was being secretive.

My brief research at Boscastle revealed that three separate people on different occasions had seen the one-eyed man in the haunted mill and none of them at that time had been aware that the building was supposed to be haunted or that a one-eyed miller had once occupied the premises.

The figure in the mist – Cannington, Somerset

I have before me a letter from Garry Bissell who tells me that when he was thirteen years of age he boarded at Brymore School of Agriculture at Cannington, and he goes on: 'It was part of our duties to look after the various animals and on one particular morning another boy and myself were on milking duty, which meant we had to get up early and fetch the cows in for milking.

'It was a cold, misty morning and at about 6.30 a.m. the cows were in a field next to two ponds. We drove them across the driveway which led up to the school. My friend was at the front and I followed them from behind. I happened to glance round and in the mist I saw a very tall figure in what appeared to be a black robe, seemingly floating towards me but I could see no face.

'I stood there totally dumbfounded and watched it get nearer and nearer until it was about fifty yards away when I got a terrible feeling of evil and foreboding; a strange wind seemed to blow all round me and the cattle started to move very quickly… I was very frightened and I ran as fast as I could past the cattle to my friend. He too had seen the figure and we both ran to the school.

'When we were both inside the milking parlour I asked my friend if he had seen what appeared to be a tall figure in a black robe but no face and he said "Yes". We agreed not to tell anyone else from the school through fear of being disbelieved and teased but all this is totally true and this I swear.

'I have no logical explanation for what we both saw but I am sure that no one tricked us. Later I found that the school is very old and over the years the property has been owned by various lords of the manor including John Pym who was, I believe, a Parliamentarian many years ago… I look forward to any possible explanation.'

The enquiries I made resulted in no plausible explanation, although several people I talked to mentioned similar experiences in the same area. The why and wherefore have yet to be discovered, but perhaps in the right atmospheric surroundings and in the presence of certain people this unidentified being might well reappear.

The ghost children – Charfield, Avon

Charfield, a rambling place on a hillside in the extreme north of Avon where the county borders with Gloucestershire, is the scene of some singular ghostly encounters. The beautiful and quiet old church with its 14th-century porch and marvellous outer door enshrines a tragic memory. In the churchyard there is a memorial to twelve victims of the Charfield railway disaster of 1928; a disaster that left behind several ghosts.

In the darkness before dawn on 13 October the night passenger and mail train shrieked its way across the foot of the Cotswolds. The passengers dozed fitfully as they waited for the train to slow down into Bristol, the end of the line and only a matter of minutes away.

Unknown to anyone aboard the express, a shunting engine was puffing its laborious way across the main line, dragging heavily-laden trucks behind it. Suddenly, amid the drizzle and fog of that early morning, a thunderous and sickening crash awakened the sleeping villagers of Charfield. Then came a nightmare of shrieking, screaming and crying as injured passengers struggled for survival amid tons of splintering woodwork and twisted and broken metalwork. And then a third train ploughed into the derailed express.

Forty-one people were badly injured, fourteen already dead. As Dr Walsingham Ward carried out his grisly examinations, searchers came across the pathetic, charred and almost unrecognisable remains of two more victims; they were small and almost certainly children. During the subsequent inquest fifteen of the dead were identified and named; two were not – one a boy of about eleven, the other a girl of perhaps seven.

The so-called Ghost Children of Charfield were never claimed; they were never reported missing, never identified. Six of the victims of the crash were buried in a grave in the old Charfield cemetery, nine others in a small plot together with the mysterious children, whose grave was inscribed 'Two Unknown'.

Conductor Harry Haines of Gloucester Station had gone through the express collecting and clipping tickets and he swore that he saw two children travelling alone in a compartment near the front of the train; one a boy of eleven or twelve, the other a girl of eight or nine. But still no one ever came forward to claim or identify the children. Someone must surely have seen them off on their journey and someone must have been expecting their arrival; it almost seemed as though they were not of this world. And as the days and weeks passed reports began to accumulate of the forms of two children, a boy and a girl, being seen in the vicinity of the crash…

Exactly a year after the crash, on 13 October 1929 to be exact, a chauffeur-driven car pulled up at the gates of the old cemetery. A woman, dressed from head to foot in black and with a thick black veil covering her face, stepped out of the car. She carried a posy of flowers which she took into the cemetery and placed on the grave marked by a memorial erected by the old London, Midland and Scottish Railway, the memorial inscribed with ten names and the evocative words: 'Two Unknown'. The woman stood for a moment looking at the grave and then she turned and hurried away. The following year she repeated her homage.

Meanwhile the people of nearby Bristol were entertained by a sensational court case involving one of their most respected citizens, Chief Constable James E Watson who, it seemed, had misused public funds by sending some of his officials on holidays as rewards for their conscientious work. Watson was suspended and eventually dismissed.

It was the same James Watson who, as part of his official duties, had played a big part in organising rescue work after the Charfield collision and who had been involved in attempts to identify the mysterious pair of children killed in the crash. At first that seemed the extent of his connection with the mystery but, when it transpired that he had disappeared, ugly whispers began to spread through the neighbourhood and further abroad.

It was suggested that the man driving the car at the cemetery had been the ex-Chief Constable and that he and the mystery woman knew more than had been revealed about the unnamed children. There was no search for James E Watson as such; after all he was a free man, but his absence added fuel to the rumours that continued to spread. Then, a couple of months after Watson had been dismissed, his great friend, a Bristol solicitor of some eminence, Francis Hapgood, received a telegram out of the blue. It read: 'Meet me at Waterloo Bridge tomorrow midnight' and it was signed, 'J. Watson'. London was 120 miles away, but Hapgood set out and met his old friend as he had been requested to do.

Apparently they shook hands, spoke briefly, shook hands again and parted. Two days later the body of James Watson was found in the pleasure gardens at Eastbourne. Nearby lay an open, cut-throat razor. The coroner recorded an 'open verdict' which seemed a little odd, to say the least, since it would appear to have been a clear case of suicide. Or were there doubts about the death? Francis Hapgood died soon afterwards and the mystery was never solved.

The lady in black was not seen again but from time to time, to this day, there are reports of the ghostly figures of two children, a boy and a girl, wandering hand in hand in the area where the frightful railway crash took place more than seventy years ago.

The boy in pyjamas – The Draynes Valley, Cornwall

Mrs Marianne Burge of Polbathic near Torpoint wrote to me as follows: 'I have just finished reading your book *Westcountry Hauntings* and felt I must write to you about an experience my husband had about six years ago.

'It was when we first moved to Cornwall and were living in a large house in the Draynes Valley, between St Cleer and Jamaica Inn at Bolventor. The house was known as Lower Langdon.

'There were two very large rooms downstairs, one we used as a bedroom and the other as a sitting-room. Upstairs were the kitchen, bathroom and another bedroom occupied by my eldest son who was then thirteen years old.

'I was in the habit of getting up several times each night to visit the bathroom upstairs (my youngest son's birth being imminent at the time). Just before my return from one such visit, my husband was lying in bed waiting for me when all of a sudden a boy aged about fifteen, appearing to be quite solid, put his head around the bedroom door and looked straight at my husband. The boy was wearing rather old-fashioned pyjamas in a blue or mauve paisley pattern.

'My husband was puzzled rather than frightened and on my return a few seconds later said, "Was that Matthew who came in just now?" If it had been Matthew, I could not have failed to have seen him as there was a long hallway and a flight of stairs from the bathroom. I had in fact checked that Matthew was asleep before coming back downstairs. In any case Matthew did not wear pyjamas in bed, just tee-shirts and shorts. My husband remarked that there was complete silence throughout the appearance of the boy, who appeared obviously taller and older than our son, in any case.

'As a matter of fact, although I never saw anything in the house, the atmosphere was unpleasant and heavy and I never liked being there on my own at night.

'A school-friend of my son's came to stay for the night some time after this incident. We had said nothing about it to Matthew as we didn't want to make him nervous. The friend went up the staircase and stood at the landing window. He went very pale and just said, "I don't want to stay here". We had to get his parents to take him home, although he never did say what he had felt or seen and we felt he didn't want to be asked.

'Finally, unrelated, but strange all the same, when I first told my brother-in-law that I was expecting our second son (who spent the first six months of his life at the house) he told me he had already dreamt the following things: that the child would be a boy, that he saw the numbers 0200 and 9.8 (which we took to be the child's birth weight), and that he would be born as the morning dew lay on the ground.

'The day my son was born, I woke up as the waters broke. I checked the time: it was exactly 2.00 a.m. My son was born at 9.08 a.m. and the nurse remarked how beautiful the morning was with the sun sparkling on the dewy grass!

'My husband has seen several other things since we moved to Cornwall, including an apparition on a building site where he was rebuilding an old house. The man was later recognised from his description, by several local residents, as a previous occupant of the house.

'Lower Langdon Farm is a large house built of granite stone block. I have only been able to discover a few facts about its past. One is a story of an elderly man who supposedly shot himself in the grounds outside; and another that in fairly recent times the house was used as a rehabilitation centre for alcoholics and tramps. No trace of a young boy has been found so far...'

In thanking Mrs Burge for her most interesting letter I asked whether the ghost boy withdrew from the doorway, disappeared where he was, or what? I also asked permission to reproduce the story in this book.

Mrs Marianne Burge was kind enough to say: '…we would be happy to have our ghost included in your book and please feel free to include any information you require.' She added: 'I believe the property may have been re-sold recently as when we last travelled past, a few changes seemed to have taken place. It would be very satisfying if the account did jog someone's memory and provided us with an explanation as to the boy's identity.'

In reply to my enquiry Mrs Burge went on: 'You ask whether the ghost withdrew out of the room, or whether it simply disappeared. My husband states that it stared straight at him, then turned and he watched it leave the room. It must have "disappeared" before I returned a few seconds later (unless I did not "see" it – although I have been interested in ghost hunting myself for a number of years and have spent nights in haunted houses, etc; unfortunately I do not believe myself to be very sensitive to them). So it may be that only my husband, who I think is very sensitive, although very matter-of-fact about it, was the only one who could "see" the boy.'

I cannot help wondering who the boy could possibly have been… perhaps a former occupant; perhaps a visitor returning to somewhere he had been happy, or unhappy; perhaps the son of a former occupant who peeped into a room one day long ago and saw – what? Perhaps the son or grandson of the man who shot himself? It is all very intriguing and I would be most interested to hear from anyone who thinks they might be able to throw any light on the mystery boy of Lower Langdon.

The persistent Miss Sarah – Falmouth, Cornwall

Miss Catherine Edwards of Falmouth wrote to me a year or two ago recounting in some detail the ghostly activity encountered there for a period extending over twenty years! I reproduce the account virtually as it was sent to me:

'Ever since I can remember I have had a tremendous interest in the supernatural, the paranormal, call it what you will. The origin of my interest was born on the first day of my arrival in our new home here twenty-two years ago.

'I was two years old when my family brought me to this house and from the beginning I was aware that we were not the only occupants of this house that I have grown to love very much.

'Naturally as a small child I would become alarmed at any occurrence that I could not understand, but as time has marched on, I have come to realise that without our faceless friends, life would not be the same.

'Allow me, if you will, to unfold some of the events that have happened to us all during our time here. The house itself was built around 1884, one of a block of four. It is an ordinary house, but at the time of its erection, it would have been viewed as a house for the middle-class, and we know for a fact that a "daily" was employed by the first occupants.

'This brings me to my next point. I carried out some enquiries as to the identity of those first occupants, the result of which supplied me with the family name and that of a sister of the then occupants, a Miss Sarah, a devout Quaker who dressed in a simple but practical fashion as befitting the time. According to the information I gained, Miss Sarah lived to a considerable age, she had a pronounced stoop and walked with a restricted shuffle.

'On my fifth birthday my mother put me to bed at six o'clock as usual and told me not to read but to go to sleep like a good girl. Since the day had been full of such new and exciting things, especially my new model pony and books, I just could not get off to sleep. So I put on my light and started to look at my new picture book. I must have been captivated by the book for some time before my interest was drawn from the book to my model pony on the cupboard beside my bed. Everything was so quiet that I can still recall the horror I felt as I watched the pony quite definitely move from one side of the cupboard to the other making an awful screeching, scraping sound as it went before falling or being flung to the ground. In my panic I could not move or say a word, let alone cry for help. After what seemed an age I managed to pull the bedclothes over my head and I remained there until I heard my mother open my door to see that all was well.

'When I tried to tell my mother what had happened she told me it must have been a draught, I must not be so silly and I must go to sleep. This incident was to be the first of many that puzzled me. On another occasion not very long after we had moved in my elder sister came to see us. Mother took her on a guided tour of the new homestead, my sister having with her a black poodle called Heidi that belonged to her mother-in-law. As the trio moved from room to room all seemed to be well until they reached the bathroom. This had once been a kitchen and a bedroom when the house had been converted into flats during the Second World War. As they approached the threshold of the bathroom Heidi began to whimper and drag her back legs. My sister tried to pull her through the door but Heidi broke free and shot down the stairs like a bullet from a gun, out through the kitchen to the safety of the back garden where my father was working in the shed.

'My sister was a little disturbed at this but carried on into the bathroom where she suddenly became aware of a presence, an icy atmosphere suddenly bringing the happy chatting to an abrupt end. Both my mother and sister looked at one another and made a hasty retreat from the room.

'On another occasion, when I had reached the age of about eight, I was again reading in my bedroom when the light went out. Not being especially put out by this, I reached out for the switch and turned it back on. It did have a tendency to do this because my father had recently redecorated my room and the

16

paint had made the switch a little stiffer than usual. As I picked up my book again the light went out once more. I was getting a little annoyed with this so once again I switched it on. It went out again and came on, went out and came on, all by itself; this went on for several seconds before I cried out for my mother.

'Mother was growing more than a little tired with my constant shouts for help during the evenings when I was supposed to be asleep, so she ran up the stairs, stormed into my bedroom and started to tell me off when the lights did their "disappearing" trick yet again. She made sure that the switch was off, closed my door and went to her own room. Moments later my light came on; not only that, the switch was making a most definite clicking sound, as if someone was flicking the switch with their finger. I cried out again but what I did not know was that my mother was experiencing the very same thing in her room next door. She came into my bedroom, held my hand and smoothed my hair until I was sound asleep. The next day my mother reported a fault in the system and an electrician called. Upon examination of the lights, wiring and switches, he announced that all was well and no repairs of any kind were required.

'Over the next two years the happenings, as we call them, were to get more regular and more spectacular. My father has a routine where he goes out every Saturday evening for a drink. About twelve years ago we always used the back door as our main entry point into the house. The front door was seldom used so we all became accustomed to the distinctive sound of the back door opening which was always preceded by the click of the latch being lifted on the back gate. Also in those days we would have our television set in the room which overlooked the back so we could always hear if anyone came in.

'However, one Saturday night, my mother, brother and myself were all sitting down watching the television. We all heard the back gate open and a man's footsteps come up the garden path, turn the handle on the back door and enter the kitchen. The time was around 9.30. We know this because mother remarked as she glanced at the clock that it was very early for father to have returned from the local. We heard the familiar sound of the coffee mugs being handled and moved; of this we took no notice, as it was my father's practice to bring coffee in for us when he came home. About twenty minutes had passed and there was still no sign of father or of the coffee, so my brother said he was going to see what Dad was up to.

'Within seconds he emerged from the kitchen, his face ashen, and he was visibly trembling; he told us that Dad was nowhere to be seen, the kettle was stone cold, the mugs unmoved and there was no sign of anyone having been in the kitchen at all.

'Dad did finally come home at around 11.00 and the first thing my mother asked him was had he returned home earlier in the evening. Of course his reply was no; in fact he had been to St Mawes on the other side of the estuary with the Nankersey choir all evening; but we had all heard our visitor in the kitchen hours earlier…

'My father was always sceptical about the whole idea that there may be ghosts in our house but he soon became a firm believer after an experience, again in the bathroom. He had gone to the bathroom for his customary evening wash and shave. During the course of his ablutions he had heard someone come up the stairs and give a sigh of relief when they reached the top. He called out, thinking it was my brother messing around, but he received no reply and thinking no more about it, he turned back to the mirror to resume his shaving when someone or something breathed down the back of his neck, releasing a mournful groan while doing so… Needless to say Dad became very alarmed and left the bathroom with some speed!

'I have also encountered a strange happening in our bathroom. It has always been rather a gloomy place but on this particular winter evening it became, just for a moment, a wonderfully warm place, filled with a happiness that I have never felt in this house before or since. I was sitting in the bath, up to my neck in foam, thinking about what I was going to do that evening, when suddenly I became aware of a presence. The hairs on my arms stood up as if a small electrical charge had been passed through my limbs, and I felt as if I was being watched. I turned my head to face the airing cupboard on my left, and there before me stood this small figure, a woman with her hair scraped back very close to her head and wearing a long navy-blue skirt, reaching nearly to the floor, and with such a small waist that she looked as though she might snap in half at the first gust of wind.

'She looked just like anyone else in the physical sense, and she was smiling but the smile forced a horrible sensation through my body as she did not appear to have any teeth. So there she was, toothless grin and all, and I could not help but notice her carriage, a pronounced stoop; all this made me feel very uneasy, but somehow the atmosphere was one of calm and I felt no urge to panic; in fact quite the opposite. I looked away and when I looked again she had gone. I remember thinking that it must be Miss Sarah and I expect she is wondering what I am doing in her house… Bearing all this in mind, I no longer took any notice of the small shadowy figure that used to shuffle past the doors on the odd wintry evening.

'We have always had great difficulty in getting animals to enter our bathroom and it has always been a great source of amusement to our friends. Whenever the opportunity presents itself for us to try and get a new dog into that bathroom without success, we become even more convinced that this must be the nerve point of all the ghostly happenings that occur in our house.

'As I moved into the next stage of my development at around thirteen years of age the activity grew stronger in our house. My father was convinced that I was the focal point for all that went on, and tried to dissuade me from delving too deeply into the unknown. I collected all the information I could on the subject and spent many hours in my room reading… I remember I had one of your books that contained many stories about hauntings in houses all over the United Kingdom.

'The noise level in our house was tremendous for about twelve months with bangings, coughs and even scratching sounds coming from the corners of the rooms. On one particular occasion during the very hot summer of 1976, I was asleep when the hatch to the attic in my bedroom slid across, causing me to be showered in grit and dust. My father said it must have been the wind but since there was not a breath of wind that night, it seemed a feeble explanation to me. This happened several times and in the end my father nailed down the hatch and put up a false ceiling to prevent it happening.

'After that our visitor took to knocking at the bedroom door, with fingernails, which was most upsetting for me. I would call out "Come in" but nobody ever did. When I went to open the door to see if it was my brother fooling about, there was never anybody in sight, the house was in darkness and everything was silent and still.

'When I was about sixteen, my brother and I took to a crude method of trying to summon up the presence using a wine glass and letters of the alphabet cut from paper. This proved to be a disaster and a month of disturbances followed, much to the annoyance of our parents.

'We eventually called in a medium whom I had befriended at the local spiritualist church. She said that the presence was a friendly one and Richard, my brother, and I were very foolish to have tried to communicate with it as we had probably called up something very unfriendly indeed.

'We followed her advice and ceased our activities; thus peace and calm returned to the house for a while. Until, that is, I purchased a harmonium. I have always loved music, especially Sankey and Moody hymns, as indeed does my father – and so it seems, does the old lady... We spent many Sunday afternoons singing around the harmonium, enjoying its mellow tones.

'On several occasions, during our Sunday afternoon sessions, we heard a woman's voice singing with us. It was quite a shock at first but now it would not be the same without her. I am now twenty-four years old; I love our house very much; and I could not think of leaving it or our friend as she has become one of the family, so to speak. It would be a terrible shame if we were to sell up and the next owners got rid of her... after all, she was here long before we were and if I have my way, she'll remain here as long as she may wish to do so.

'As for the manly footsteps; well, we have not heard them since I was a small girl and I don't suppose we'll ever know who they belonged to. There have been many other happenings in this house, some nice and some not so nice. But whenever they happen at least now we are not at all bothered by them; indeed life would be very mundane and ordinary without them.'

In reply I said, 'How interesting that you seem to have ghostly activity that is confined to the house and its occupants and I am pleased to know that like most people in similar circumstances, you have come to terms with whatever entities there may be and live in harmony with them; ghostly encounters notwithstanding.'

The Grey Lady – Exeter, Devon

The old Royal Devon and Exeter Hospital in Southernhay, Exeter, renamed Dean Clarke House, has a famous Grey Lady ghost which has haunted the hospital for many years.

The hospital, which dates back to 1741, was left a forlorn shadow of its former self in 1974, when all the doctors, nurses and patients moved away to the new general hospital at Wonford.

They left behind just a few caretakers – and the Grey Lady who, according to tradition, haunts the first floor corridor of the oldest part of the building. Until the early part of the 20th century, matrons of the hospital slept in a bedroom served by the corridor, and it is said that generations of nurses and doctors saw the ghost there.

She is known as the 'Grey Lady' because of the grey uniform of an 18th century nursing sister that she is supposed to wear. Tradition says that she was always running along the corridor whenever anyone saw her.

If by chance she felt lonely for a while she can be lonely no more, for the old hospital sprang back to life in 1977 as the headquarters of the Exeter Health Care District, and the Treasury of the Devon Area Health Authority, and nearly two hundred staff moved in.

The associate administrator of the Exeter Health Care District, Mr Alan Ruddock, said at the time: 'We have not seen the ghost yet, but we have heard a good deal about her. Her presence does not really bother us.'

Mrs Molly Alford, a former administrative sister, retired after thirty-six years of nursing in the hospital, said she had heard a good deal about the ghost too, but she had never seen her personally. Miss Ruth Furze, a former matron, confirmed that until shortly after the Second World War the matron's bedroom was on the supposedly haunted corridor.

If the Grey Lady has not been seen in recent years, said Miss Furze, it was possible that she was smoked out by a fire which badly damaged the floor above in 1968. However, since I never heard of a ghost being destroyed by fire or even put off by smoke, I am not surprised to hear that the Grey Lady has in fact been seen several times in recent years.

A former nursing sister tells me that she saw the ghost one evening in 1973. At the time she recalls being struck by two things: firstly, the 'nurse' ahead of her in the long corridor was running – something nurses are taught not to do, and secondly, the 'nurse' was dressed all wrong – she was wearing a grey out-dated uniform… This informant tells me that as these points went through her mind, the figure suddenly vanished and for the first time the viewer felt uneasy, frightened almost, for there was no way in which the figure could have disappeared from sight naturally.

Another witness I talked to, a former nurse, told me she had an almost identical experience some twenty years earlier. I understand that the 'haunted' corridor is now much changed but apparently the ghost still walks or rather runs on occasions in her accustomed place.

The grieving ghost – Newton Abbot, Devon

A lady living near Exeter read my book *Ghosts of Devon* and says it inspired her to relate her experiences while living at Newton Abbot some twenty years ago. She writes:

'When my husband and I moved from Salcombe to Newton Abbot I was six months pregnant and my initial "uneasiness" about the house was put down to my being unwell during this time. With hindsight, the whole house had a very musty, old smell to it even though it had been re-decorated prior to our moving in; also, when standing in the hallway our eyes were invariably drawn upstairs as if a "shadow had moved…"

'We chose the bedroom at the front of the house, putting our little daughter into the adjoining back bedroom. Invariably she woke some time in the night to say our Labrador was in her room – mistakenly.

'When our second daughter was about six months old, we put both little girls in the same room, hoping Julia would sleep more contentedly; but no – she still had disturbed nights. We then thought of actually changing bedrooms and this had the desired effect.

'Then, one night towards the end of one of my husband's weeks of night duty, I awakened to find "someone" quite solid standing at one side of our bed dressed in a white sweater. I was extremely cold and it was deathly quiet, even when "it" crossed its arms in front to take the sweater off!! There was no sound whatever. Even though I knew it was not my husband I still said, "Is that you?" and "it" looked at me – it seemed to have "floppy" cheeks I remember – and then it disappeared. I could see our wardrobe again…

'My husband arrived home less than an hour later. I ran downstairs and told him what had happened. He, like me, was in no doubt that I had seen a ghost…

'A few months later we had an elderly lady medium come to the house to see whether she could tell us anything about "our friend". By the time she reached our upstairs landing she was crying her heart out and later she said it was a very strong experience. Apparently "he" was grieving all the time for his mother who had been buried in Highweek Cemetery, and he would go from the vicinity of our spare bedroom through our bathroom to the back bedroom (where originally our daughters had slept and now, my husband and myself) and look out longingly at that place.

'She also said "his" house was a large old red-brick place with a corridor where our bedroom was now situated; but our house had only been built for approximately ten years at that time. Apparently he would also sit downstairs, she said, pointing to a corner of our sitting room, still grieving, and looking towards Highweek.

'The only little bit of research we did was to try and find out about the original house, the one that we supposed had once occupied the site before our house was built; but we were told there was no such place… Then, about twelve months later, South Western Electricity Board decided to demolish their cooling tower which was situated across the mud flats from the back of our house and there, in direct line and now visible from our back bedroom, was Highweek Cemetery. The medium told us too that the ghost's name was Rupert Williams; perhaps I'll do some research into that one day…'

On the road – Nunney, Somerset

At a meeting of The Ghost Club Society, which was addressed by Michael Goss on the subject of 'The Evidence for Phantom Hitch-hikers', we talked about the curious Nunney case.

Three miles southwest of Frome, the attractive little village has become something of a mecca for would-be ghost-seers after a 'middle-aged' phantom was repeatedly reported to be seeking to hitch lifts on the road leading to Frome – and then disappearing.

An early report came from a 20-year-old decorator who claimed he had picked up a man wearing a check jacket on the Frome-Nunney road. The man had climbed into the back seat of the car and the driver locked the door on him. Apparently the only remark made by the traveller was to the coldness of the weather. Almost immediately a question from the driver elicited no response and, when he turned round, he found the traveller had disappeared although he had heard no sound of any kind. The puzzled driver, worried that his unidentified passenger might have been injured alighting from a moving car, reported the matter to the local police – who promptly gave him a breathalyser test: he had not been drinking.

Shortly afterwards the same young man claimed to have undergone a second encounter with the same individual – at approximately the same place. This time the 'middle-aged man' was standing in the middle of the road and the driver had to skid to a sudden halt when he came upon the 'man'. When he got out of his car the person he had clearly seen, and recognised as the man to whom he had previously given a lift, had completely disappeared.

News of this second encounter and further stories of somewhat dubious origin prompted local residents to form what came to be called the Nunney Vigilantes who patrolled the area with noise detectors, tape recorders, light meters and cameras, under the leadership of Ron Macey (who actually lived on the haunted road) but, perhaps predictably, they had no success in obtaining evidence of the 'phantom hitch-hiker'.

The local police then came forward with news of an accident resulting from a driver swerving to avoid a man in the road and they readily admitted that on 'several occasions' drivers had arrived at the police station 'in a state of virtual hysteria' to report vanishing figures on the same stretch of road. Police and local residents were intrigued by the idea that the 'hitch-hiker' might be the ghost of an American serviceman killed in a car crash in the identical area.

Margaret Royal told me that she traced three separate motorists who, late at night, had picked up a man who subsequently inexplicably vanished on the Nunney road. One had reported the matter at Frome Police Station and another had gone to hospital for treatment for shock. Each motorist referred to the 'man' as 'between forty and fifty and wearing a check jacket'.

At the height of the publicity surrounding the appearances a former lorry-driver, George Gardiner, came forward to reveal that years earlier he could recall one or two of his fellow drivers reporting seeing what might well have been the same ghostly figure in the same area of roadway. He added that his understanding at the time had been that a cyclist had been knocked down by a motorist at the 'haunted' spot and his appearance was the result of his dying curse on all motorists.

Mr Owen Hillier, a resident of Nunney for over fifty years, said he had heard his father talk of the ghost and, he believed, his father's father too. His recollection was that the ghost appearances concerned an innocent man hanged for the murder of his wife.

Whatever the explanation, 'frequent' reports of vanishing hitch-hikers on this stretch of road resulted in several police searches being made along the road – all unfruitful.

The Nunney case is a good illustration of how very difficult it can be to establish a ghost sighting, but if we feel there is no unassailable evidence that the Frome to Nunney road was ever haunted in the way reported then we are left with the awkward question of why motorists would attempt to hoax the police with so unlikely a tale as that of a vanishing passenger – and all so convincingly that the police instigated searches and preserved reports. Similar conflicting evidence pervades many reported ghostly encounters.

A wistful ghost – Blackawton, Devon

If the ruins of haunted Oldstone Hall in Blackawton, a quiet South Hams hamlet, could talk they would tell of murder as well as ghostly encounters.

The hall was completed in the early days of the 18th century, being built on the site of a monastery by the Cholwich family, local wool merchants, who lived here for many years. It was a beautiful house in those days, with three lakes in the grounds, a grotto, several secret tunnels and a hermit's cave – traces of all these can still be found. However the Cholwich family fell upon hard times and the house was sold to Percy Dimes, who had once been a steward of the Cholwiches.

Such are the twists of fate. It was while Percy Dimes was enjoying the life of a squire that a terrible disaster occurred.

Dimes' beautiful daughter, Laura, fell in love with a young New Zealander named Hugh Shortland who was training to become a barrister, but he did not find favour with Laura's parents.

Mr and Mrs Dimes were not convinced that the plausible, dashing and admittedly presentable immigrant was a good match for their daughter and they forbade Hugh to enter the grounds of Oldstone Hall. Soon the couple were meeting clandestinely in nearby woods where they strolled hand in hand beside Monk's Pond. And soon they married secretly with Laura still living with her parents, certain that she would eventually be able to talk them round to accepting Hugh.

One day, after taking her home after a ride, Hugh left her as usual at the gates of the Hall and Laura wandered off into the woods for a walk by herself – and she never returned. Hours later, during a search, her riding hat was seen seemingly floating a few inches above the waters of Monk's Pond, quite near the bank. Then her drowned body was found, bolt upright, beneath the hat and soon Hugh Shortland was arrested on suspicion of murder. At the resulting trial he defended himself brilliantly; he was acquitted and the mystery of Laura's death was never solved.

The sudden, mysterious and untimely death of Laura hit her family hard. The house never seemed the same without her and in fact the family always said that she hadn't really left; everyone, without exception, was convinced that the ghost of Laura Dimes haunted the house she loved. Even a visiting chimney sweep saw the ghost of Laura Dimes in what became known as The Ghost Room.

Ten years after Laura's death a mysterious fire destroyed Oldstone Hall and the only room left intact was The Ghost Room. Today her ghost haunts the ruins of the house where once she was happy. People living nearby are convinced they have seen Laura's ghost, perhaps seeking retribution for her murder; perhaps seeking to right some wrong that she had done; perhaps looking for the love of her life.

Whatever the reason, those who have encountered the ghost of Laura Dimes at Oldstone Hall seem to become affected with the wistful sadness that seemingly exudes from this lonely apparition in her lonely haunt.

The soldier spirit – Southleigh, Devon

Some fifteen years ago a family named Downs moved from Yorkshire to their new home in Southleigh, Devon. Nicholas Downs, wine producer, his wife Helen, son Ian and daughters Sheena and Emma all soon realised that they had moved into a haunted 17th-century farmhouse.

Teenager Sheena was the first to say she was aware of a 'presence' in the house; shortly afterwards her younger sister Emma noticed it too and then Mrs Helen Downs became aware of 'something' in the house other than the human occupants. The family pet dog had acted strangely ever since they had moved in, frequently acting as though it was aware of something invisible to its human companions. And then it refused to enter one room where the family felt the ghost lingered.

One day a visitor, who had not been told of the odd feelings experienced by the occupants of the house, suddenly described a frightening encounter with a man dressed in old-fashioned military uniform... and then there was the night when Sheena was awakened at three o'clock in the morning by the sound of heavy breathing which continued, close to her, until she switched on her bedside lamp. The breathing sound ceased immediately and there was nothing to account for what she had heard.

Two weeks later Sheena's mother had an almost identical experience. Then one night, also at three o'clock in the morning, Emma revealed that she had been awakened by a weight pressing on her stomach. When she put her light on she saw that a heavy picture had been moved across the room while she had been asleep; a few nights later she was again awakened about the same time and as she switched on the lamp she saw a book 'floating through the air…'

The dog became more and more agitated in the vicinity of the bedroom where some of the disturbances took place and a presence there was felt by all the family; Emma in particular 'became a bag of nerves' (to quote her mother). 'She is frightened of being alone anywhere upstairs,' she said at the time and decided that it might be best if the girls slept together.

That same night Emma awoke again at three o'clock with the feeling of a dreadful weight on her chest. She awakened Sheena who said afterwards: 'We heard a curious, high-pitched sound, like you get from a radio that is not tuned in… I sat up and shouted at the ghost to leave Emma alone. Almost immediately I was slapped hard across the face…'

The family called in a priest from Exeter. The Reverend John Wheaton of the Liberal Catholic Church performed a two-hour exorcism and cleansing ceremony – and the haunting completely ceased.

Mr Wheaton said afterwards: 'We were dealing with the spirit of a human being who had been dead for a hundred years or more – a long-dead soldier. I severed the chains which were keeping him captive to the house where he once lived.' It was a ghostly encounter that Sheena and Emma Downs would always remember.

The ghost of a murderer – Zennor, Cornwall

I have in my records firsthand evidence for some very strange happenings in a cottage on Zennor Moors.

Some months after the family moved into the large cottage not too far from Penzance they began to realise that they could not simply disregard drawings and messages that appeared mysteriously and unaccountably on the wall by the stairway. One of the curious facts (comparable with the wall writings that appeared at Borley Rectory, 'the most haunted house in England', when the paranormal activity there was at its height) is that while no one in the family was above five feet nine inches in height, none of the drawings and messages were less than five feet eleven inches high.

As the writings continued, articles in the house, and especially articles with religious associations such as a crucifix and some black beads, would be moved or would disappear completely.

Friends staying with the family would sometimes complain of curious sensations, such as a burning feeling in the toes. One witness said it felt just as though a lighted match had been placed under the toes, but after a moment the sensation completely vanished. Several visitors reported this, none aware that the identical sensation had been experienced previously by other people. And that applied equally to the strange smells.

These smells seemed to be confined to one particular corner of one bedroom and different people described the smells differently: as resembling stale cheese, blood, sweat and human urine.

In an adjoining room, occupied by two sisters in their twenties, voices were heard. Although no actual words were distinguishable, the tone and apparent urgency of the sounds were very frightening; as was the occasion when the son of the family awoke one night to find blood on his palm. He was unable to sleep alone in the room for several nights thereafter.

Other incidents observed or experienced by members of the family and by visitors included the smashing of the glass front of a clock and the movement of some coins (in one instance some of the missing coins were found inside the battery section of a tape recorder) and the definite but never observed movement of objects placed on an old beam in the cottage.

One seemingly impossible transportation concerned a large boiler which stood beside a door. The boiler was in fact larger than the doorway, yet it was found one morning in the adjoining room having seemingly passed through a hole too small to take its bulk!

Other disturbances included rapping sounds and voices in various parts of the cottage, some of which were recorded on tape; and an indistinct figure was seen standing in the kitchen doorway.

Curiously enough, a few months after receiving one report on this case I received another from an entirely different source but reporting very similar activity in the same area. Here some form of contact seems to have been made with the ill-defined figure that lingered in a doorway. It was established to the satisfaction of the people concerned that a former resident had been responsible for the death of someone in the 'haunted' bedroom and was seeking to draw attention to the fact in the hope of obtaining peace.

After considerable research, and patient and sympathetic involvement with the entity, the disturbances abated. When I last heard from this family they had experienced nothing untoward for several weeks and were holding their breath in the hope that their sincere wish to help the unhappy haunter had in fact freed it from any necessity for further encounters in the Cornish cottage.